W9-AOU-042

WITHDRAWN

How People Lived

How People Lived in

Ancient
Greece

Colin Hynson

PowerKiDS
press.

New York

Published in 2009 by The Rosen Publishing Group Inc.
29 East 21st Street, New York, NY 10010

First Edition

Library of Congress Cataloging-in-Publication Data

Hynson, Colin.
  How people lived in ancient Greece / Colin Hynson.
     p. cm. — (How people lived)
  Includes index.
  ISBN 978-1-4042-4431-3 (library binding)
  ISBN 978-1-4358-2621-2 (paperback)
  ISBN 978-1-4358-2635-9 (6-pack)
 1. Greece—Social life and customs—Juvenile literature. I. Title.
  DF78.H96 2009
  938—dc22
                                             2007040219

Cover (main image): A statue from the eighth century B.C. of the famous Greek poet, Homer.
He is shown wearing a long piece of cloth called a himation.

Picture acknowledgments: Alinari/Topfoto: 11; Courtesy of the Trustees of the British Museum
London: 13br; British Museum London/HIP/Topfoto: front cover inset b, 5, 9, 24; Peter
Connolly/AKG Images: front cover inset c, 8; Bob Daemmrich/Image Works/Topfoto: 27; Rainer
Hackenburg/AKG Images: 6; David Lees/Corbis: front cover inset t, 13bl; Erich Lessing/Musée du
Louvre Paris/AKG Images: 12, 15, 16, 18, 19, 22, 26; Erich Lessing/Museo Archaeologico
Nazionale Chiusi/AKG Images: 21; Erich Lessing/Museum of Fine Arts Boston/AKG Images: 14;
Nimatallah/Agora Museum Athens/AKG Images: 10; Nimatallah/Museo Nazionale Archaeologico
Naples/AKG Images: front cover main, 23; Picturepoint/Topham: 17; Ann Ronan Picture
Library/HIP/Topfoto: 20; Topfoto: 25.

Map by Peter Bull.

Manufactured in China

Contents

Words that appear in **bold**
can be found in the glossary
on page 28.

WHO WERE THE ANCIENT GREEKS?

The Ancient Greeks lived over 26 centuries ago, during what many people think is one of the most important periods in history. From Ancient Greek times came many very important things that we take for granted today. For example, a lot of the words that we use in our languages in Europe can be traced to Ancient Greece. Ideas from that time about politics, art, buildings, and literature still influence us.

Many buildings, such as the Supreme Court in Washington, D.C. and the British Museum in England, use Greek ideas about architecture. Our modern **democracies** come from Greek ideas about politics.

▲ The main entrance to the walled city of Mycenae was the Lion Gate. It was built in about 1250 B.C.

THE ORIGINS OF THE GREEKS

The Ancient Greek civilization arose from earlier groups of people that made their homes in Greece. The two most important were the **Minoans** and the **Mycenaeans**. The Minoans lived on the Greek island of Crete between 2200 and 1400 B.C. They traded all over the Mediterranean and built the magnificent palace of Knossos. The warlike Mycenaeans lived on the Greek mainland. By 1600 B.C., they controlled a large part of Greece. However, by about 1200 B.C., they had been attacked and destroyed by the Dorian people, who came from the north of Greece. With the end of the Mycenaean civilization, Greece entered a "dark age." It took about three hundred years for Ancient Greece to rise out of this "dark age" and create a new civilization.

EXPANSION OVERSEAS

As Ancient Greece became more prosperous and towns and cities began to expand, the population throughout Greece began to increase. The hot climate and mountainous geography of Greece meant that the people could not grow enough to feed everyone. From about 1000 B.C., many Greeks left their homes to start a new life in places around the Mediterranean. They settled in areas that are now Italy, Cyprus, Tunisia, and Turkey.

▶ This map shows the main city-states of Ancient Greece in about 600 B.C. It also shows where the Ancient Greeks settled in modern-day Turkey.

THE "GOLDEN AGE" OF ANCIENT GREECE

Greece was not a single country but was split into several **city-states**. These were areas of land that were controlled by a large city. The "golden age" was the time when Ancient Greek civilization was seen to be at its greatest. This happened in around the fifth century B.C. in the city-state of Athens.

ANCIENT GREEK TIMELINE

200 B.C.	2000	1800	1600	1400	1200	1000	800	600	400 B.C.

2200–1400 B.C.
The rise of the Minoans on the island of Crete.

1600 B.C.
The Myceneans control a large part of Greece.

1200 B.C.
The Myceneans are conquered by the Dorian people.

1200–900 B.C.
Greece goes through a "dark age."

1000 B.C.
Greek people begin to leave their homes for new areas.

500 B.C.
The "golden age" of Ancient Greece.

ANCIENT GREEK MEN, WOMEN, AND CHILDREN

Although the city-states (see page 7) of Ancient Greece were powerful and prosperous, that power and prosperity was not equally shared among the people. The wealthy had a lot more power than the poor. Adults had many more freedoms than children, and men were allowed to do much more than women. **Slaves** in Ancient Greece had much less power and wealth than those who were free.

▼ Greek men had to spend some of their time in the army. This fifth century B.C. vase painting shows soldiers putting on their armor.

MEN IN ANCIENT GREECE

Men had the most power in Ancient Greece. Only men were allowed to take part in the government. The city-states of Athens and Sparta both had **assemblies** (see page 10) in which all male **citizens** could become part of the government. Ancient Greek men did not spend much time at home, since they were often out working or away fighting in the army.

WOMEN IN ANCIENT GREECE

Ancient Greek women had very little freedom and few rights. They could not leave home without being accompanied and were not allowed to take part in the decisions of the city-state. After a woman was married, she was put in charge of running the house, either giving slaves orders or doing the jobs herself. The women of Sparta had more rights than other women. They were allowed to own their own property and could even marry another man if their husbands were away from home for too long.

▼ This small statue shows a Spartan woman taking part in a running race (see page 24). The women of Sparta were trained to be strong and athletic.

CHILDREN IN ANCIENT GREECE

It was only boys from wealthy families who were sent to school in Ancient Greece. Wealthy girls usually had a private tutor at home. Children from poorer families had no education at all. Boys learned a trade or joined the army, and girls were taught how to cook, weave clothes, and run a home.

REAL LIVES

SAPPHO: A FAMOUS POET

One of the most famous women from Ancient Greece was Sappho. She was born in 650 B.C. on the island of Lesbos. She came from a wealthy family, and she was taught to read, write, and play music. She was a poet who influenced many Greek writers such as Plato. Some historians believe that she also invented the plectrum, a kind of pick, to play the **lyre**.

WHO WAS IN CHARGE IN ANCIENT GREECE?

By the eighth century B.C., Greece began to emerge out of what has been called a "dark age" (see pages 6–7). The rulers of the larger cities began to control large parts of the land that surrounded each city. These areas were known as city-states. Each city-state was called a polis (which is where our word *politics* comes from). The most important of these were Sparta and Athens. At first, they were controlled by a handful of the most wealthy families, and there were often struggles for power between them. By the middle of the sixth century B.C., Cleisthenes, the ruler of Athens, created a new form of government in which citizens could participate. However, only male citizens were allowed to take part. Women, slaves, and foreigners were excluded. The Spartans followed the Athenians with their own assembly but did not give it as many powers.

THE ASSEMBLY IN ATHENS

The assembly was the most important part of Athenian government. It decided on all new laws. The assembly was made up of all male citizens over the age of 18. It met every ten days on a hill called the Phyx. At least 6,000 citizens had to be present and everybody had a right to speak.

◄▲These four pieces of broken pottery have the name of the Athenian politician, Themistocles. He was exiled in 470 B.C.

EXILING POLITICIANS

In Athens, members of the assembly could vote to get rid of unpopular fellow members. They would scratch a name on a piece of broken pottery called an **ostrakon**. The names were then counted. If there was a large enough vote against one man, he would be exiled (or "ostracized") from Athens for ten years.

THE GOVERNMENT OF SPARTA

The Spartans had two kings who shared power. Below them was a council of 28 nobles. The members of this council all had to be over 60 years old, and they decided on the policies of Sparta. An assembly of all males born in Sparta selected the council. The council was run by a small group of men called the **ephorate**.

WOMEN IN CHARGE?

Women were excluded from taking part in the assemblies in both Athens and Sparta. However, some women had a degree of influence, especially in Sparta, where women were allowed to have their own property. Men could only become part of the assembly if both their mothers and fathers were citizens.

REAL LIVES

ASPASIA: A POWERFUL SPEECHWRITER

Aspasia, shown here, lived in Athens in about 440 B.C. She was one of the most powerful women in Ancient Greece. She lived with a statesman called Perikles and is thought to have written some of his speeches. She was admired by other Greek writers, such as Plutarch. He wrote that she "managed as she pleased the foremost men of the state" with her intellect and knowledge.

WHAT WAS LIFE LIKE IN AN ANCIENT GREEK FAMILY?

For the people of Ancient Greece, marriage and having children was seen as their most important duty to the city-state. In every city-state, married couples were expected to have plenty of children who would later become soldiers, workers, and parents. Households were generally quite large. A married couple and their children lived together with other relatives, such as elderly parents or unmarried sisters. In Athens, the average age for a man to die was 45 years and for a woman, 36 years. This meant that very few children still had both parents living by the time they reached adulthood.

▲ The painting on this fifth century B.C. vase shows a bride being led to her new house.

GETTING MARRIED

The average age to get married in Athens was about 15 years for women and about 30 for men. Neither of them had any choice about who they could marry. The decision was normally made by their fathers. However, they usually married people that they already knew. It was possible to marry a cousin, uncle or a father's close friend. Marrying for love was rare and was not approved of.

An important part of the marriage ceremony was when the bride was led in a procession to her new house. She was followed by her mother, her new husband, and his best friend. There was also a long line of musicians and well-wishers.

HAVING A BABY

The arrival of a baby was a time of great joy. When the baby was five days old, it was carried naked around the hearth of the house by the father and was then considered to be a proper part of the family. Names were given when the baby was ten days old. The first-born boy was given his grandfather's name.

In Sparta, only healthy babies were allowed to survive. When a baby was just a few days old, its father took it to the council of 28 nobles (see page 11). If the baby was strong, then it was taken home. If it was considered to be a sick or a weak baby, it was taken to the mountains and left to die.

▼ The arrival of a baby was a time of celebration. This carving shows a baby being presented to its grandmother.

▲ This vase painting shows an Ancient Greek baby sitting on a very large potty.

ANCIENT GREEK HOMES

The homes of the Ancient Greeks were made of bricks made from dried mud, and the floors were usually made of beaten clay or earth. These houses have long since disappeared, because in time, they just crumbled to dust. However, a few of the homes of wealthier families have survived, because they were built of stronger materials such as stone.

THE LAYOUT OF AN ANCIENT GREEK HOME

Most Ancient Greek homes that belonged to wealthy people had a courtyard. All the main rooms within the house faced toward the courtyard. The rooms had very small windows, which helped to keep them cool in the summer. The house was built in such a way that the men, women, and children had their own areas where they slept, ate, and entertained.

WOMEN AT HOME

The area of the house set aside for women was called the **gynaeceum**. It was usually located at the back of the house. However, women were expected to look after the entire household. If they had slaves, then the women made sure that they were working properly. Poorer women had to do all the household chores by themselves.

▲ One of a woman's household tasks was to make sure that the family's clothes were clean. This painting shows a woman washing some clothes.

MEN AT HOME

Men were not expected to be at home very much. When they were there, they would conduct business and entertain their friends. The part of the house set aside for men was called the **andron**. It was usually on the north side of the courtyard, so that it could catch the warmth of the winter sun.

CHILDREN AT HOME

Children were usually looked after by their mothers, so they spent a lot of their time in the gynaeceum. The courtyard was an important area for children because it was a safe place to play. Children were not allowed to enter the andron. When a boy was 12 or 13 years old, he was considered old enough to join his father there.

▲ The baby in this statue is being held by its mother. It is wrapped in swaddling clothes to help keep it still.

REAL LIVES

XENOPHON: ADVISING WOMEN ON MANAGING THE HOME

In the fourth century B.C., an Ancient Greek male historian named Xenophon wrote a book called *Household Management*, which was supposed to be read by women. In it, he wrote: "You must stay indoors and send out slaves whose work is outside. Those who remain and do chores inside the house are under your charge."

DID ANCIENT GREEK CHILDREN GO TO SCHOOL?

In theory, education in Ancient Greece was available to every child, but in practice, only the wealthiest families could afford to educate their children. If a child did go to school, that meant they were not at home helping with household chores, or even earning a living. The Ancient Greeks believed that only boys needed to be educated. Girls were not expected to go to school, because they were needed at home to help take care of the house and to prepare for marriage. In Sparta, the state paid for, and provided, the education of all boys in order to prepare them to become warriors.

GOING TO SCHOOL

The sons of wealthy families went to school from the age of seven to 18. They usually had three teachers. One taught them reading, writing, mathematics, and literature. The boys were supposed to learn long passages of poetry by heart. These were usually stories of brave deeds and daring adventures. Another teacher taught sports, such as wrestling, athletics, and gymnastics. The third teacher was a music master, who taught singing and how to play instruments such as the lyre.

▲ One of the reasons why girls were taught to play a musical instrument was to entertain men during banquets. This vase painting shows a woman playing the pipes.

THE EDUCATION OF GIRLS

Ancient Greek girls did not go to school but stayed at home and learned household skills, such as weaving, from their mothers. The girls of wealthy families sometimes had teachers who came to their homes to teach them to read and write, or to play a musical instrument. They used these skills to entertain the rest of the family, particularly during a **symposium**. A symposium was a party during which men feasted, had discussions, and recited poetry. Only men could take part.

Education in Sparta

The rulers of Sparta wanted to make sure that they always had a strong army to defend the city-state. Every boy was taken from his family at the age of seven and was sent to live in an army barracks. The boys learned a little reading and writing, but most of their time was spent in physical exercise and learning military drill. Life for these boys was very hard. For instance, they were deliberately kept hungry and were encouraged to steal food. This taught them how to survive during times of war. If they were caught, then they were beaten. This was not for taking the food but for getting caught. We still use the word *spartan* to describe something that is very simple or strict.

Just like their brothers, all Spartan girls were taken from their families at the age of seven and were trained in different sports. They even trained with the boys. The Spartans wanted girls to become healthy women, so they could then have strong sons who would grow up to become good soldiers.

◀ Training to be soldier was the most important part of a Spartan boy's education. This statue is of a soldier with a shield and helmet.

WHAT JOBS DID THE ANCIENT GREEKS DO?

Ancient Greek men often had little choice about the jobs they could do. As boys, they simply learned the same trade as their father and then continued when they were adults. Most people either worked in farming or fishing. Many men also had to join the army during times of war, and spend months—or even years—away from home. The only kind of work that women were allowed to do was in the home, although poorer women would have helped with farming. The Ancient Greeks relied on slaves to do a lot of the work.

ANCIENT GREEK FISHING

Fish was one of the most important dishes in an Ancient Greek meal, and many people ate it at least once a day. This meant that many of the Greek men who lived next to the sea were involved in fishing. The seas around Greece had large numbers of tuna, mackerel, squid, and octopus. Fishermen set sail in small wooden boats and caught the fish with nets and spears. Although fishing was hard work, the seas around Greece were usually very calm, so it was not viewed as a dangerous job.

▲ Preparing food was a job for poor women or female slaves. This woman is kneading dough before she bakes it into bread.

ANCIENT GREEK FARMING

The Ancient Greeks relied on small, family-run farms to grow their food. Wheat and barley were grown for making bread. Other important crops included peas, beans, grapes, olives, and apples. Farmers had no machinery to help them with growing and harvesting their crops. The wheat and barley was gathered by hand. Slaves worked on larger farms. On smaller farms, every member of the family was expected to help. Fruit crops had to be picked from the trees, although there is some evidence that monkeys were trained to pick olives.

▼ The Ancient Greeks often used oxen to pull their plows. The man on the right is sowing seeds from a bag slung around his shoulder.

IN THE ARMY

Many Greek men had to join the army in time of war, and even had to pay for their own armor and weapons. Ordinary soldiers were called **hoplites**. Their weapons were a spear and a sword, and their armor was usually made of bronze and leather. The Spartan army was the most feared, because Spartan men spent their whole time in the army and were considered ferocious fighters.

SLAVERY IN ANCIENT GREECE

Much of the hard work in Ancient Greece was done by slaves. Slaves were usually prisoners of war, but some, particularly children, were sold into slavery by poor families. Female and child slaves helped to look after the homes of wealthy Greeks. Male slaves did heavier work, including dangerous jobs, such as digging in silver mines at Laurion in Attica, a region in southeast Greece that surrounds Athens.

ANCIENT GREEK CRAFTS

The Ancient Greeks became famous for producing many fine crafts. The objects that craftspeople created, such as pottery and woven cloth, were supposed to be useful, but were also made to look beautiful. The city-states of Greece were known for different kinds of craftwork. For example, Athens was famous for pottery and Corinth was celebrated for its metalwork, especially gold and silver work. Women throughout Greece knew how to weave. Weaving was a skill they were taught as girls. It was considered an essential part of their domestic duties.

► This funeral wreath of flowers and leaves is made from fine pieces of gold. It was made between 350 and 325 B.C. for a king of Macedonia.

ANCIENT GREEK POTTERY

The pottery of Athens was sold all over Ancient Greece. It was famous because the clay used to make the pots would turn a warm brown color after it had been fired. Many of the potters worked in an area of Athens called the "Kerameikos." In the fifth century B.C., there were about 500 potters working in this area. Only a few potters' names survive and all of these are male.

ANCIENT GREEK METALWORK

Corinth was best known for the quality of its metalwork, particularly its fine jewelry. Greek women wore jewelry, because it showed how wealthy their family was. Ordinary jewelry was made from cheaper metals, such as tin, copper, and lead. Wealthy Greek women could afford jewelry made of silver or gold decorated with fine threads of gold and jewels.

WEAVING AND SPINNING AT HOME

Weaving was the one job that women were allowed to do by themselves. Every Ancient Greek home had a loom to weave wool into cloth. Before this was done, the wool had to be cleaned and dyed. This was a messy job and it was done in the courtyard. The cloth was then turned into clothes and furnishings for the house. Poorer women would sell some of their weaving in their local marketplace, called the **agora**.

▶ This man and woman are in front of a loom. The weaving on the loom is decorated with mythical animals, such as a flying horse named Pegasus.

REAL LIVES

EUTHYMIDES AND EUPHRONIUS: RIVAL POTTERS

In the late sixth century B.C., there was a potter named Euthymides. He was admired for the way that he painted figures on his pots. He usually wrote "Euthymides painted me" on his pots. He had a rival potter named Euphronius. On one of his pots, Euthymides wrote "Euphronius never did anything like this."

WHAT DID THE ANCIENT GREEK PEOPLE WEAR?

▲ This young woman is holding a mirror in one hand and a makeup box in the other. She is wearing the sleeveless *peplos*.

Although there were many differences in the lives of men, women, and children in Ancient Greece, in one respect they were more or less the same. Everyone wore very similar clothing. Children just had smaller versions of the clothes their mothers and fathers wore. The Ancient Greeks believed that wearing plain, simple clothing would show people that the wearer led a pure and virtuous life.

THE CLOTHES FOR WOMEN AND GIRLS

The most popular piece of clothing for women in eighth century B.C. was the **peplos**. This was a long, sleeveless tunic made of wool. It was held together with pins on each shoulder and a belt around the waist. By the middle of the sixth century B.C., the peplos had been replaced by the **chiton**. It had loose sleeves and was held in place with pins along the sleeves. The chiton was made of linen and was lighter than the peplos.

THE CLOTHES FOR MEN AND BOYS

The most basic item of clothing for Ancient Greek men and boys was the **exomis**. This was a tunic that just covered the knees. It was mostly worn by workers and slaves. Men and boys also wore the chiton, but in winter they could keep warm by wearing a **himation** instead. This was a long piece of cloth that was wrapped around the body and then thrown over the shoulder.

JEWELRY AND HAIRSTYLES

If clothing was the same for everybody, rich people could show off their wealth in other ways. Wealthy women wore plenty of richly decorated jewelry, and had different hairstyles with hairbands and tiaras. Having long hair was a sign that a woman did not have to work. The only piece of jewelry worn by men was a signet ring.

▲ This is an eighth century B.C. statue of a famous Greek poet named Homer. He is wearing a himation.

SIMON: A SHOEMAKER

The fifth-century writer, Socrates, used to visit the shops around the marketplace in Athens to talk to the shopkeepers who worked there. He wrote about a shoemaker named Simon, whose shop was in the southwest corner of the marketplace. A friend of Socrates wrote that Simon was "a virtuous man but a bad shoemaker."

HOW DID PEOPLE HAVE FUN IN ANCIENT GREECE?

People in Ancient Greece often stopped work to enjoy themselves. The time to have fun was often part of a festival to honor a god or goddess. Festivals were celebrated with processions, singing, dancing, and drinking. One of the most important festivals, held every four years, was the Olympic Games. Going to the theater was an important part of Ancient Greek life. The children of wealthy parents had expensive toys and games bought for them. Other Greek children did have some toys, but these were homemade or bought very cheaply.

THE OLYMPIC GAMES

The Ancient Greeks believed that sports were an important way of honoring the gods. All the city-states sent athletes to Olympia to take part in chariot races, athletics, and field sports, such as throwing the discus and taking part in the long jump. Wars were suspended so that every athlete could travel safely to Olympia. The games lasted for five days and large crowds would watch.

▲ These two young women are playing a game of knucklebones, or jacks.

WOMEN AT THE GAMES

Women were not allowed to watch or to take part in the Olympics. However, unmarried women were allowed to come to some of the events to look for a husband (although their choice still had to be approved by their father). Women had their own festival at Olympia called the Heraia. There was only one event and that was a running race. It was divided up so that girls and women could run with others who were the same age.

GOING TO THE THEATER

Plays in Ancient Greece were held in large open-air theaters. Some of these theaters were so large, they could seat 14,000 people at one time. The plays were usually **comedies** or **tragedies**. Women were not allowed to act, so men had to play female parts as well. Women were allowed to watch plays but were generally discouraged from going to the theater, because it was not considered proper for women to go out in public.

▲ The theater at Epidauros was designed so that everybody could have a good view of the stage.

PLAYING AT HOME

Babies were given clay rattles to play with. From vase paintings, we know that boys played with small carts and tiny boats. Girls were given wooden dolls or played a game called "knucklebones," like modern-day jacks. A small set of bones was thrown into the air and caught on the back of the hand. Whoever managed to catch the most pieces was the winner. Because it used pieces of bone, which could be found for free, knucklebones was played by poorer Greek children, too.

REAL LIVES

MILON OF CROTON: AN OLYMPIC ATHLETE

One of the best-known Olympic athletes was Milon of Croton, who lived in the late sixth century B.C. He was a well-known wrestler and won six victories at the Olympic Games. The Greek historian, Diodorus Siculus, wrote that Milon would wear his Olympic wreaths when he went into battle.

HOW IMPORTANT WAS RELIGION FOR THE ANCIENT GREEKS?

The Ancient Greeks worshipped many different gods and goddesses. People believed that the gods took a real interest in their day-to-day lives and could influence what happened to them. They believed that if the gods were pleased, they would help people and answer their prayers. Worshiping of the gods took place at home and in magnificent stone temples. Men, women, and children took part in worship.

GODS AND GODDESSES

Each of the gods and goddesses worshiped by the Ancient Greeks had control over one aspect of the world. The king of the gods was Zeus. Other gods included Apollo, the god of light, truth, and agriculture, and Ares, the god of war. Goddesses included: Athena, the goddess of wisdom; Aphrodite, the goddess of love; and Hera, the goddess of marriage.

▲ This man and woman are pouring either wine or olive oil over an altar as an offering to the gods.

WORSHIPPING THE GODS

For most Ancient Greeks, worship started at home. There was a small altar that was usually placed in the courtyard. The whole family, including slaves, would worship at the altar. Burnt offerings and even the sacrifice of small animals would take place here.

Worship at a temple was usually part of a festival. Every god or goddess had their own separate festival. There were also festivals for special occasions, such as victory in battle. At these festivals, a large number of people worshiped together. Each temple was dedicated to a particular god or goddess. The main temple dedicated to Apollo was at Delphi. The **Parthenon** was built on the Acropolis in Athens. It was used to worship Athena.

WOMEN AND RELIGION

In Ancient Greek temples, the worship of gods was led by priests and the worship of the goddesses by priestesses. This meant that women had a very important part to play in worship and festivals. The priestesses at the Parthenon were important figures in Athens, because they were viewed as the link between the gods and the people of Athens. The chief priestess at the Parthenon was called the **Pythia**. It was believed that the Pythia could predict the future.

▲ The Parthenon building was the most important temple on the Acropolis in Athens.

CHILDREN AND RELIGION

Each spring, a festival called Anthestria was held to honor the god Dionysus. Every boy who had reached his third birthday was brought to a temple and given his first sip of wine. There was also an annual festival called Apaturia to which new-born babies were brought to be blessed. Girls had an important role in festivals. They washed statues of the gods and made special cakes as offerings.

Glossary

agora An open marketplace.

andron A small dining area where men would entertain their friends.

assembly A gathering of citizens to make decisions about how the city-state should be run.

chiton The most common form of clothing in Ancient Greece, which was worn by men, women, and children.

citizen An adult, native-born member of a city-state.

city-state A city that controlled a large area of land around it.

comedy A type of play that is supposed to make people laugh and has a happy ending.

democracy A city-state that was controlled by the adult males, who were also citizens.

ephorate A small council of men that helped to run the city-state of Sparta.

exomis A type of tunic, mostly worn by male workers and slaves.

gynaeceum The part of the house set aside for women and girls.

himation A cloak worn by men and boys to keep them warm.

hoplite A Greek foot soldier.

lyre A musical instrument, like a harp, with strings.

Minoan An early civilization on the island of Crete.

Mycenaean An early civilization on mainland Greece.

ostrakon A piece of pottery on which members of the assembly could write down the name of another member they wanted to banish.

Parthenon A temple at the Acropolis in Athens that was dedicated to the goddess Athena.

peplos A long, sleeveless tunic made of wool, fastened at the shoulder and belted around the waist.

Pythia The chief priestess at the Parthenon.

slave A person who was not free and was not a citizen of Ancient Greece.

symposium A party in which only men could take part, during which feasting and discussions took place.

tragedy A type of play that deals with more serious themes than a comedy and has an unhappy ending.

FURTHER INFORMATION

BOOKS TO READ

If I Were a Kid in Ancient Greece
(Cricket Books, 2007)

Peter Ackroyd
Ancient Greece
(DK Children, 2005)

Chris Chelepi
Growing Up in Ancient Greece
(Troll Communications, 1993)

Sally Hewitt and Ruth Thomson
The Greeks
(Franklin Watts, 2001)

Colin Hynson
Find Out About Ancient Greece
(Wayland, 2006)

Fiona MacDonald
Women in Ancient Greece
(Peter Bedrick, 1999)

Anne Pearson
Everyday Life in Ancient Greece
(Sea to Sea Publications, 2005)

Richard Tames
Ancient Greek Children
(Heinemann, 2002)

Web Sites

Due to the changing nature of Internet links, PowerKids Press has developed an online list of Web Sites related to the subject of this book. This site is regularly updated. Please use this link to access this list: www.powerkidslinks.com/hpl/greece

Index

Numbers in **bold** indicate pictures.